The Most Insane Historical Rulers

Top Mad and Crazy Rulers from BCE to 20th century

Benjamin J. Brown

Table of Contents

Introduction

Throughout history, and across the world, there have been dozens of great empires, plenty of powerful and mighty civilizations, kingdoms, countries and regions, and each and every one has been overseen by leaders of great influence and strength. Many of these leaders were kindly, wise, just and benevolent characters, adored by their people and respected by their peers. Indeed, most countries still celebrate the finest of their historic leaders, and fondly remember the good they did for their country and countryfolk. The ancient past was a difficult time in every corner of the world; the introduction of cross-border trade, the constant need to gather precious resources, and the inherent human spirit of competition meant that there were often skirmishes and wars between neighboring countries. However, as these countries grew, as their populations expanded and became more demanding, more and more power was given to leaders and kings, who were often heads of religion and heads of military forces.

More power inevitably leads to more corruption, and absolute power can quickly send men and women mad. As such, it comes as no surprise to find that world history is littered with leaders, emperors, kings and queens who were nothing less than insane – despotic, selfish, power-hungry and obsessed with vice and self-abasement. Generally speaking, their insanity was born of cruelty and excess, but of course, in many cases the ruling classes were made up of 'pure' bloodlines, meaning clinical insanity brought about from incest and inbreeding was also often commonplace.

When researching and studying mad, evil and megalomaniacal rulers of the past, we must try to approach the subject with a sense of fairness and balance. Often, history is not kind to particular leaders, portraying those who wished for change as insane, or allowing them to become victims of nasty propaganda campaigns. However, there are also doubtlessly genuine examples of the truly wicked, the truly vicious and cruel. There are more than enough historical records which show the sheer numbers who had to die at the hands of an emperor's whim, and many of them have been proven reliable, or they at least give a good idea of the extent of particular leader's capacity for cruelty. But in each and every case recorded in this text, there are two sides to a story. While a leader may have been responsible for the deaths of thousands of innocent men and women, there will always be those who consider their actions as important, or valuable, or even just. Repressed nations grew into mighty empires at the point of a sword, and continents were transformed into the forms we see them today with the blood of nations.

Here we have gathered twenty examples of historical rulers; from warlords to emperors, queens to military commanders, most of them have displayed unique capacities for sadism, cruelty and in some cases, genuine madness and insanity. These are all people who had an enormous impact on history and on world geography; borders shifted as a result of their rule, empires rose and fell again, and they are all people with valuable lessons to teach which are still relevant to this day. Their stories are fascinating, and have given us many of the most colorful legends and stories we have to tell, and yet the fact that such stories are true makes them all the more interesting, and all the more terrifying.

Nero (AD 37 - 68)

When it comes to historical examples of evil, insane, despotic and megalomaniacal rulers, there is only really one civilization that stands head and shoulders above the rest. The Roman Empire was, and remains, one of the truly great examples of an ancient system built on power and politics, and while it paved the way for modern life and society as we know it with all its inventiveness and brilliance, it also provided us with many of the most astonishing and shocking examples of madness in leadership the world has ever seen. Thanks to the reams of records produced in this time by great diarists, satirists, playwrights, poets and reporters, historians now have quite a clear and complete picture of the excesses and evils committed by Rome's all-powerful leaders, many of whom were a mess of contradictions. On the one hand, many of these emperors oversaw the development of one of the most successful world powers history has ever known, and on the other, often the same ruling individuals were clearly insane, unspeakably cruel and sadistic, and capable of genuine atrocity. One of the most fascinating and enduring examples of such extremity is

Nero – a man who developed many of the artistic and political ideals the Romans are still celebrated for, and yet also murdered, tortured and destroyed almost all around him within his lifetime. Nero lives on today through many artistic depictions of his evil and excess, and while myths have grown up around him, the truth of his madness can still shock and appall.

Nero was born Lucius Domitius Ahenobarbus in AD 37, in a noble family celebrated by the ruling classes for their military achievements. However, when Nero was just a child, his mother, the formidable and ambitious Agrippina, was exiled by Emperor Caligula to the Pontian Islands, along with her children. However, after a few years in exile, Caligula was killed and Claudius took the throne. Claudius, compared to his predecessor, was a mild and sensible ruler, and quickly pardoned and recalled Agrippina back to Rome. On her return, Agrippina seduced and married Claudius, and demanded that he adopt her son (who was given the name Nero by his stepfather), and provide him with the best education Rome had to offer a growing boy of noble blood. Nero was tutored by the legendary philosopher Seneca, and developed a keen interest in the arts - particularly music - and politics. By the time Nero was a teenager, his hunger for power and excess began to show. His mother set about trying to influence her husband politically and financially, and when he resisted, she most probably had him poisoned by one of her lovers. For a short while, Agrippina took control of the late Claudius' empire, but within months she was kicked aside by her own son, who refused to share power with anyone in his family. A long and bizarre rivalry between mother and son commenced, something which many historians speculate was the true root of Nero's insanity.

Interestingly enough, despite his reputation, Nero was actually a fine leader in his early years. Unlike many of his predecessors, he diligently applied himself to his role, taking on many different tasks instead of relying on courtiers and advisers, and continuing many of the humane acts Claudius had introduced. Indeed, Nero actually banned gladiatorial games under his early rule, as he claimed they had no place in a civilized society such as Rome. His tutor, Seneca, had taught him well, and the young Nero was a sensitive ruler, desperate to avoid bloodshed as much as possible. However, as he grew older, he was forced by his role and by his family to make increasingly difficult and emotionally challenging decisions, and it was after he had to put four hundred slaves to death that he began to withdraw from political life, and devote himself to his growing appetite for theatre, music, sex and sadism. His withdrawal signaled the end of his humane rule, as his position was now open to influence by corrupt senators, advisers and military leaders.

Despite being married to Claudius' daughter, Octavia, Nero had many lovers – many of whom were commoners and not of the court. His mother became wildly jealous of two of his mistresses, and violently opposed his relationships with other women. Nero's derangement was increasing daily, and he set about personally trying to murder his mother, who, bizarrely, survived two poisoning attempts, her bedroom ceiling collapsing onto her bed, and a deliberate boating accident designed to drown her. Nero finally succeeded in the murder of his mother with the help of assassins, who clubbed her to death in AD 59. With his controlling mother gone, and almost all of his duties as emperor now handed over to others, Nero was free to indulge himself – and indulge he most certainly did. Wild sadistic orgies took place in the palace and on the streets, in which he reported dressed in the skins of lions, and murdered prostitutes and young boys. He raped and killed whoever he pleased, and forced audiences of thousands to endure long theatrical and musical recitals, of which he was the unquestioned star. One report even state that he forced an arena full of citizens to stay and watch him perform a play which continued for days, with armed guards ensuring nobody could leave. Apparently, women gave birth within the Amphitheatre, and healthy men pretended to die in order to be carried away. Nero also famously competed – and won - in chariot races and a Roman version of the Olympic games, in which he repeatedly fell off his chariot, but had promised to murder anyone who tried to overtake him.

As he grew older, the excesses became increasingly destructive, and his people turned against him ever more. Rome burned in a mighty fire, and Nero was seen atop a tower, singing wildly into the flames (not playing the fiddle as in artistic depictions of the scene). He required a useful scapegoat, to take the blame for his disastrous rule, and focused all his energy on vilifying the newly emergent sect of Christianity. These Christians were kidnapped from all corners of the empire, and were tortured and executed in appalling ways – from being broken on wheels, to crucifixion, and even forced fighting in the gladiatorial games he had once banned. He also used live Christians as 'human torches' during his orgies, burning them alive to provide light and heat for his guests as they ate, danced, and committed their own atrocities.

Eventually, the opposition to Nero's rule of

insanity and sadism grew stronger and stronger, and when he was sentenced to death by his own senate, he took his own life to avoid the certain painful death he faced at the hands of his people. His own last words sum up his utter self-delusion: "What a great artist the world has lost in me".

Commodus (AD 161 - 192)

Throughout history, many empires and

civilizations have risen and fallen, leaving space for new powers and ideologies to arise. Each of these civilizations were overseen and ruled by a wide range of charismatic leaders, from philosopher kings, living gods, warriors and tyrants. However, the one civilization which managed to be at once the seat of the most brilliant and innovative minds, as well as the most deranged and maniacal despots is undoubtedly that of the Romans – a vast and all-powerful conquering force which eventually began to crumble and collapse after centuries of madness, incest, corruption and pure evil at the very top of the social and political system. There were many, many insane rulers of the Roman Empire, spread over many hundreds of years. However, arguably the most disastrous (certainly from a political perspective), and amongst the most deranged and ridiculous was Emperor Commodus.

To say that Commodus turned out to be a disappointment to his people and peers would be enormous understatement. He was the son of Marcus Aurelius, perhaps the wisest, most politically and tactically successful emperor the empire had seen, and a gifted philosopher who largely had the love and respect of his subjects. Indeed, Aurelius' masterwork; *Meditations,* is still held up today as a fine example of ancient philosophy and historical interpretive writing. Commodus was expected to better his father, to continue the wisdom and success Rome and the empire had enjoyed under his leadership. But it seemed to many that Commodus was somehow sinister and untrustworthy from the moment he was born; the only surviving child of fourteen siblings, all of whose brothers and sisters died (some suspiciously) before they reached adulthood. Nonetheless, Commodus was crowned as Caesar (the equivalent of junior emperor) at the age of five, a move which many felt was odd, even by Roman standards. Eleven years later, when Commodus was sixteen, he was crowned joint-emperor, now having been groomed and deemed ready to rule alongside his father.

The early rule of Commodus was mostly spent traveling alongside Marcus Aurelius, on various military campaigns throughout central Europe, defeating Germanic tribes and conquering large swathes of densely forested land, thus expanding the already enormous and formidable empire they oversaw. He saw plenty of success, as well as murder, rape and other such crimes of war alongside the banks of the Danube during these years, as well as attempted rebellion within his own ranks. Many historians credit this period as formative in the young man's life – for all his father's wisdom, the young Commodus was undoubtedly exposed to atrocities in his teens, and was invited to celebrate in the murder and destruction of hundreds, if not thousands, of people. As well as this, during this time away, generals and soldiers of high rank who kept Commodus' company began to comment on the voracious appetite for vice and excess displayed by the co-Emperor, and word began to spread that Rome may have a 'new Nero' on her hands. However, it seems as though Commodus' behavior was largely kept in check (or at least well hidden) while Marcus Aurelius continued to reign.

Of course, Marcus Aurelius' reign was never going to last forever, and when he died in AD 180, the almighty power of the Roman Empire was passed onto his only surviving child, Commodus. With his father now gone, and with the world at his feet, Commodus saw the empire as his playground, open and inviting him to delve as deep into corruption, insanity and cruelty as he pleased. The fact is, Commodus was a terrible emperor, a monster and megalomaniac who failed disastrously in almost everything his father had succeeded in. Huge chunks of the empire were lost in poorly conceived military campaigns, peace treaties were broken and avenged upon, and a large proportion of the empire's riches were squandered on vanity projects, palaces and arenas built solely for the precocious leader's enjoyment and distraction. As with Nero before him, Commodus quickly lost interest in the job he inherited once he discovered his capacity for cruelty, sadism and sex. Most of the governing work and leadership was passed onto Commodus' chief of security, nicknamed 'The Dagger', who, as one might expect, had little experience of running an empire and as such made many, many costly errors. Meanwhile, Commodus spent his time with his vast harem, said to contain three hundred young women, and three hundred young slave boys, who he raped and tortured, and occasionally killed, whenever he pleased. Naturally, it wasn't long before rebellions started to break out, and one of the first assassination attempts was organized by his own sister, who he promptly put to death and displayed publicly as an example to any potential traitors.

As he grew older, Commodus became increasingly vain, increasingly erratic and dangerous, and increasingly insane. He renamed the city of Rome after himself, named months of the year after himself, and transformed the imperial palaces into gladiatorial arenas. Indeed, fighting, wrestling and gladiatorial games grew into Commodus' main obsession, and it is perhaps this he is best remembered for. He repeatedly demanded to perform in the amphitheaters of Rome as a gladiator, much to the shame and hilarity of his subjects. In this time, those forced into the ring under fear of execution were primarily the lowest members of society; criminals, prostitutes, traitors and Christians. For the Roman people to see their ultimate ruler, their emperor, taking on such a role would have been utterly scandalous, and would have left no doubt in the public's mind that here stood a man incapable of bringing any further glory to the empire. Furthermore, Commodus' forays into the arena were utterly embarrassing in more ways than one. Firstly, he would dress as the Roman mythical hero, Hercules, and parade around the ring dressed in a loincloth and lion skin. On top of this, his opponents were said to be either crippled prior to the competition, or tied to the spot, or equipped with useless wooden weapons which offered them no defense. Commodus was reported to have killed one hundred bears in a single game within the gladiatorial ring – an impressive feat, were it not for the fact that the bears were chained to posts and lanced by the emperor from a distance. As the public, the senate and the ruling classes became more and more disgusted and disappointed in their clearly insane leader, it wasn't long before several assassination attempts were made, the final one seeing Commodus strangled in his bed by his wrestling partner.

Vlad III (1431 - 1476)

Few names in history have resounded for as long, or struck terror into the hearts and minds of as many as that of Vlad III of Wallachia. If this name is unfamiliar to you, then one of his many monikers – Vlad Dracul, Vlad Tepes, Dracula or Vlad the Impaler – may help you recognize this most bloodthirsty, sadistic and tyrannical of European rulers. Indeed, his infamy and notoriety has lived on through the ages due to the fact that his story and character spawned many myths and legends, perhaps most notably in the key horror novel of the 19th century; Bram Stoker's *Dracula*. While the fictional Count Dracula was a supernatural being, capable of hypnosis, shape-shifting and crawling down vertical castle walls, the reality behind the legend is no less shocking, and manages to even surpass Stoker's vampire when it comes to extremes of cruelty and insanity. Today, the historical figure of Vlad III remains a subject of much fascination to history fans and thrill-seekers around the world, and his ancestral home in central Romania has become an important tourist attraction for those keen to uncover the monstrous secrets and blood-soaked acts committed by a man who, despite the evils he committed, helped shape central Europe as we know it.

The name 'Dracul' or 'Dracula' is always going to be an evocative one, and the story behind this most terrifying of titles is not only fascinating, but gives us some idea about the identity of Vlad III, and the way in which he was viewed in his lifetime. Interestingly, the name comes from two sources, and can be understood in two separate ways. Firstly, Vlad's father, Vlad II, adopted the name Dracul (meaning *dragon*) as a reference to his family crest. The dragon referred to a specific order set up by the 15th century king of Hungary and Holy Roman Emperor, created to fight the invading Turkish armies, who were steadily creeping their way across eastern Europe at this time, pillaging towns and extending their already huge and powerful empire. The Order of the Dragon was an elite tactical and military force, and Vlad II was appointed an elder of the order as a result of his valor in battle, and later, when he became ruler of the kingdom of Wallachia (now central

Romania), he used the dragon as his official emblem, with the symbol appearing on coats of arms, coins and other such standards of his rule. His son, Vlad III, readily continued the use of his father's crest when he succeeded him to power. However, 'Dracul' also means 'devil' in Romanian, and Vlad III's obvious sadism and ruthlessness as a ruler led to his people and his enemies using this word alongside his name as an accurate description of his character.

At the beginning of his reign, Vlad III was something of a necessary evil for the kingdom of Wallachia. The region was a highly contested part of Europe, battled over for centuries. On one side, Catholic Hungary was growing quickly and powerfully, extending its borders into modern day Romania, Ukraine and the rest of the Balkans. On the other, the vast, rich Ottoman Empire was rampaging through both Eastern and Southern Europe, spreading Islam with a more technically gifted, dedicated and ruthless army. Vlad III had to play a careful political game with both sides, in order to maintain the sovereignty of his land, and is even remembered happily by certain Romanians for standing up to the Ottomans and stopping them in their tracks for a period of time.

Nobody really knows when Vlad III's thirst for blood and cruelty began, but many would claim that his childhood – surrounded by political assassinations, warfare and sacrifice – would have a huge impact on his later life. Furthermore, the young Vlad Dracul was himself used as a political tool, given away as a hostage by his own father to the Turks for many years as a way of pacifying the encroaching armies from the east. What happened to Vlad while in the city of Adrianople remains a mystery, but upon his release, he returned to Wallachia twisted, corrupt, and with a violent ambition for leadership and vengeance. Although he was next in line to the throne of his kingdom, Vlad was quick to kill off any competition, and once in power, set on a campaign to display his might and warn any potential enemies that he was not a leader to be taken lightly, or trifled with.

Of course, in such a troubled region, Vlad III was constantly having to deal with invaders, as well as unrest within his own country. However, it is the method in which he chose to deal with such troublemakers which has really given him the fearsome reputation he is best known for. Vlad III executed thousands upon thousands of his enemies, and he did so via one of the most gruesome and agonizing methods history has ever known. Traitors to his kingdom, and enemies from the east would be hoisted upon tall stakes, and impaled – ensuring a slow, painful and utterly disgusting death, visible for all to see as a warning to those within Wallachia, and as a method to terrify and disgust any invaders from abroad. Records show that the stakes used were oiled, and ensured to be slightly rounded at the point. If it were too sharp, the victim would die quickly of shock. Instead, the blunted stake would be inserted through the anus, gradually using the force of gravity to push its way through the body, exiting at the throat or through the chest. The stakes were erected in concentric circles around the city limits, with important victims (for example, generals or ambassadors) on taller stakes to reflect their status and in order to make an example of them. What is truly astonishing about these executions, though, was the horrendous numbers in which they were carried out. When Mohammed II of the newly conquered Constantinople rode to Wallachia in 1461, he was greeted at the city of Tirgoviste by the sight of twenty thousand impaled Turkish soldiers. This great warrior and leader was reduced to a quivering wreck within what became known as The Forest of The Dead. Records also tell of St. Bartholomew's Day in 1459, one of the most blood-soaked moments in Romanian history. On this religious feast day, Vlad The Impaler is said to have feasted in the shadow of thirty thousand impaled merchants and innocents from Transylvania, reveling in the destruction and cruelty his power granted him.

Despite these monstrous displays of power, the Turks eventually overpowered Wallachia, and Vlad fled the country in 1462, where he was arrested by the King of Hungary and placed into a royal tower. However, over time, he regained the king's favor, and even married a member of the Hungarian royal household, who gave birth to two sons. Astonishingly, many of the royal families of modern Europe – including the British house of Windsor – can claim to be direct descendants of this bizarre union, and most terrifying of leaders.

Herod (74 BCE – 4 BCE)

There are certain historical leaders who have, over time, become more than mere people. Through storytelling, legend, religion and speculation, they descend beyond evil to the status of villain, or cultural bogeyman. Every great world religion has at least one of these figures – a living, human antithesis to goodness, a nemesis to a hero or paragon of virtue. These individuals often end up being plot devices, or dangerous messages in morality, existing to teach the faithful the dangers of turning one's back on virtue. Perhaps the most famous of these characters is King Herod, the king of the Jews in the time of Christ's birth and Jesus' first enemy. While we must be careful when studying characters from religious stories – due to the fact that they are often exaggerated or simply invented in order to add color to a story – there are often shocking and true facts behind the tale. The true story of Herod is somewhat shrouded in mystery, but historians and theologists have pieced together the reality of this biblical villain, and we now know him to be a complicated leader, whose evil actions and paranoid delusions helped form civilization as we know it today.

Herod was a man of Arabic origin, but had converted to Judaism early in his life – partly due to family pressure, and partly because it offered him an easier route to power. He was born in the year 74 BCE, the son of wealthy nobles who wielded plenty of power in the region, and he was raised to gain plenty of power of his own. Cunning and brutal, he rose through the ranks as a teenager, until at the age of twenty-five he became governor of Galilee and began experiencing the kind of power which would eventually overtake his senses and lead him to commit his famous atrocities. These were times of great turmoil and nastiness, and it wasn't long before rivals usurped Herod's family, causing Herod to flee to Rome where he knew he would be supported on his returning mission of vengeance. He was granted money and his own army, and he returned to Judea with the intention of overthrowing the new leaders, and murdering all of those who stood in his way. His mission was successful, and after several gruesome assassinations, Herod was granted the title 'King of the Jews' by the Roman senate. He decided to expand his power and favor over the Jewish people who treated him with extreme suspicion (indeed, the Pharisees refused to even acknowledge the fact that he considered himself Jewish) by marrying into the noble family of Antigonus, but there was one problem – Herod was already married to a woman named Doris, and they had a son. However, Herod displayed his brutality by banishing them both on fear of death. He further demonstrated his callousness and power hunger by executing his father-in-law, the king of Judea, and taking his throne in order to begin his own royal dynasty.

The occupying Roman forces in the land which is now Palestine clearly viewed him as a formidable leader, keen to wipe out the civil unrest that existed in his region with military force. This is exactly what he did, and from a political perspective, his rule was extremely successful. His kingdom was extended into Syria and Jordan, at much human cost. Herod, however, cared little for human life – he was mainly preoccupied with building lavish temples and spending all his subject's money on the creation of palaces, making him increasingly unpopular and hated by the Jews he supposedly reigned over. Indeed, all of his building projects meant that he was constantly raising taxes in Judea, squeezing the last pennies out of an impoverished community, who were bitterly angry with their decadent ruler. Any attempts to question his rule, or rebel against him, however, were immediately trampled by Herod and his vicious secret guard, who terrorized the public and executed hundreds – no wonder so many of the Jewish people of Judea began to see him as a monster.

Herod's most famous act of evil is, of course, recorded in the gospel of Matthew, in the New Testament. The 'massacre of the innocents' was uniquely an evil act, inspired by paranoia and a desperate bid to maintain power in an increasingly angry kingdom. According to the text, the Three Magi visited Herod's palace in order to inform him that the astrological signs pointed towards the coming of a new king, the prophesied savior of the Jewish people who would depose the enemies of Judaism and rescue the lands in which he was born. As we all know, Herod was then said to personally oversee the execution of all babies born within Bethlehem and the surrounding regions, in an attempt to kill the coming savior before he could grow up and defeat him. There are plenty of debate regarding the authenticity of this story, not least because the gospel of Matthew is the only place it can be found. It is most likely a composite story, partly taken from other, similar birth stories of other, similar deities (indeed, there was a massacre of the innocents committed by King Kamsa in India, when the birth of Krishna was foretold), and partly from reality. Herod was certainly capable of murder, and had killed his own two sons in order to ensure he remained in power. He also murdered his beloved wife, after growing suspicious of her and her family, believing they were plotting to overthrow him. There is no doubt that Herod was a despot and a dictator, driven by mania and paranoia, and even his death was cruel and bizarre. When he knew that he was dying, he was so worried that nobody would mourn him that he ordered the murder of dozens of distinguished men in Jericho, in order to create a chaotic display of public grief at the same time as his passing in 4BCE. However, whether or not he was guilty of many of the crimes attributed to him is still open for debate, and will possible remain this way forever.

Mary I (1516 -1558)

The English monarchic system is one which stretches back almost a thousand years, to when the Norman king, William, successfully invaded England in 1066 and took the title of King of the realm. Before him, the whole of the United Kingdom was split into separate kingdoms, constantly plotting and scheming against each other, and as such, a unified country was always going to be a stronger, more durable system. However, for over six hundred years, it allowed absolute power to single heads of state, opening up the system to corruption, cruelty, and occasional madness. It wasn't until the English civil war in the 17th century that the complete power of the monarchy was taken away and handed over to parliament, and by then, England and what would become the United Kingdom of Great Britain and Northern Ireland had seen more than its fair share of evil and corrupt leaders. Mary I stands out in many ways when we consider the country's worst monarchs, for many interesting reasons. She had the almost impossible job of being the first ever female queen of England, a country hitherto ruled by powerful and charismatic men, and she ruled in a time of unimaginable levels of religious reform, something which had plunged England into a state of chaos. Over time, and due to her constant poor judgment, growing paranoia and selfishness, she became the most notorious and hated monarch the country had ever seen, and will forever be known by her notorious nickname 'Bloody Mary'.

Mary's childhood was a difficult one, and her young life was a constant whirlpool of conflicts and hatred which perhaps influenced her later, hateful decisions against her own people. Her father was the formidable Henry VIII, perhaps the most famous of England's Tudor monarchs, and her mother, the Spanish queen Catherine of Aragon. Her mother was Henry's first wife, who he grew to despise and fear – partly for her coldness and loyalty to Spain, and partly for the fact she consistently failed to bear him a son. This particular problem led Henry to divorce his wife, something which would change British history forever. In order to separate from the woman he could no longer abide, he was forced to split with the power of Rome, and declare his kingdom an independent, protestant country, with he the leader of the state religion. Because of his frustrations with Catherine and her inability to bear a male heir, much of Henry's frustration was projected towards his daughter, the young Mary. She embodied his failings with his first wife, and he shunned her - the heir to the throne - while pursuing a further five wives. Mary grew up miserably with her mother, but more significantly, she grew up Catholic. Meanwhile, the Church of England was being formed, and Catholics across the country were being persecuted, their abbeys, monasteries and churches destroyed and ransacked for their treasures.

What is particularly interesting about Mary is the fact that she probably never even considered that she would become Queen. When Henry bore a son, after having not one but two daughters, the country celebrated as the girls were forgotten. However, when Henry died and his son Edward took the throne as a teenager, he became one of the shortest living monarchs in English history, succumbing to disease before he reached twenty. At this point, the only other Tudor heirs were Mary, and her half-sister Elizabeth. Mary, being the elder, was crowned as the first queen of England, and she approached her throne full of hatred, anger and revenge, vowing to restore Catholicism to England, to avenge her father for the neglect and cruelty he had shown Mary and her mother, and to punish and kill those who wished the religion and laws of her father to continue.

Almost instantly, Mary was an utter disaster as a queen. She felt more loyalty to Spain than to England, a country which the English were almost constantly at war with. She married her cousin, King Philip of Spain, and the fact that a Spaniard was technically king of England threw the country into chaos. Mary responded in a typically vengeful manner, throwing anyone she suspected of treachery against her husband into the tower to be executed, and taking advice of Spanish advisers, keen to see the downfall of England. However, it was her Catholicism which really caused problems. She saw every single English protestant as a traitor and potential murderer, and quickly set about arranging them to be executed. In a particularly sick twist, her preferred method of execution was public burning at the stake, and hundreds upon hundreds of priests, reformers, and ordinary members of the public were gruesomely burned as heretics in every town square in the country. This was a considerable step back for England, which was on the edge of a Golden Age before Mary took power with all her insanity and burning anger.

Her hatred wasn't merely extended to the protestant community, though. She also despised members of her own family, and signed death warrants against her cousin, the beloved Jane Grey, whom Henry had personally promised the throne before he died. Both she and her husband were beheaded, with their heads on display over London for weeks. She also imprisoned her sister, Elizabeth, who remained either inside the Tower of London, or under house arrest during the entire of Mary's reign. The only reason she didn't behead Elizabeth alongside the hundreds of others who met that fate was because she knew it would spark a civil war. By the time Mary died in 1558, England was a country on its knees due to religious and political unrest. Huge sums of money had been wasted, or stolen by the Spanish, court officials and nobles had been infected by Mary's paranoia and madness, and England was more vulnerable than it had been in hundreds of years. Thankfully, she died childless, and her sister Elizabeth ascended to the throne, while Philip skulked back to Spain.

Empress Wu Zetian (c.625 – 705)

There have been precious few female rulers in any country throughout history, as men have held on to seats of power more or less since civilization began. Indeed, the very systems of monarchy and inheritance have more or less always been angled in favor of the masculine, with divine rights, kingdoms and empires being handed down from father to son, or being won on the battlefield at the point of a sword. However, the few female rulers who reigned in both the east and west are often the ones who had the greatest impact on a country, and it could even be fair to say (in Europe, at least) that many of the most successful eras of the most successful countries were brought about by female hands. Women rulers have almost always been deeply controversial, though, with opinion on their rule varying wildly depending on whose point of view you take. Historians must be very careful when studying the stories of queens and empresses, as more often than not, their rules were followed by centuries-long smear campaigns, waged by the kings and emperors who came after them. Certainly, one of the most controversial queens of antiquity can be found in the old empire of China, where male rule was absolute for centuries. However, in the seventh century, a remarkable, beautiful and charismatic woman rose to power – somebody who undoubtedly committed atrocities against her family, her people and her enemies, and whose ambition for power meant certain death for anyone who stood in her way.

Empress Wu Zetian was, in many ways, a remarkable woman. She was born in 662 AD in China with the name Li Dan, from a relatively lowly family. However, she was groomed from childhood to catch the attention of the imperial court, and her radiant beauty saw her introduced to the emperor as a concubine. In those days, concubines were expected to be utterly subservient to their masters, but the fact that they had to strive to attain their much-feted position meant that the harems they lived in were hives of competition, nastiness and ruthless behavior between the teenage girls. It has been suggested and rumored that the young Li Dan, who by that point had changed her name to Wu Zhao, was responsible for the murder or mutilation of more than one of her concubine peers, although this may be little more than hearsay. What is unquestionable, though, is that she quickly became the most important concubine in the palace, and was favored by the emperor's father, and soon after by the emperor himself. Many historians have claimed that her ability to seduce the emperor was based on her own sadism, and was the only woman capable of satisfying the emperor's more bizarre and masochistic sexual requests.

Wu was not happy to be mere harem-girl, though, and set her eye firmly on the throne. She faced one huge blockade to her ambitions, however – the emperor's wife, Wang, who was a highly influential figure in the empire. Wu Zhao formulated a plan, which was monstrous as it was cunning. She allowed herself to fall pregnant (possibly by the emperor, but sources vary), and upon the birth of her baby, she smothered and suffocated it, and set up a complex case in which Wang – the queen herself – was framed for the crime. Wang was imprisoned in appalling conditions on charges of murder and treason, but this was not enough for Wu, who ordered her to be tortured, mutilated and eventually drowned in a vat of wine. With the empress out of the way, Wu could take the royal name of Zetian, and rule as empress in her place.

However, there was still much work for Wu to do. The emperor already had children from his previous marriage, and these sons were set to inherit the empire when he died. This was simply not part of Wu's plan for all-out power and domination, and so she had them killed, placing her own children as the next in line. Furthermore, she feared her own family would try and take some of her power, or try to muscle in and influence her, or even steal from her, and she had most of her relatives put to death, exiled, tortured and disgraced. Her determination went further still, as she systematically ordered the executions of all twelve branches of the royal family, effectively wiping out an entire dynasty who had a claim to the throne. Her mother was poisoned, her older brother dismembered, and eventually, her husband, the emperor, succumbed to her murderous wishes. This is noted in history as being peculiar for the fact that his death was alone, unobserved, and unceremonious – something unthinkable in Chinese royal tradition, and something which scarred the noble classes deeply at the time.

As she grew older, scandal surrounding Wu Zetian grew and grew. She attempted to deify herself, allowing Buddhism to flourish in China due to their female deities, which she imposed herself upon and ordered temples to enshrine images of herself alongside their gods and goddesses. She took many lovers, and was reportedly still sexually insatiable until her death. What must be noted, however, is that despite her cruelty and eccentricities, Wu as an empress was actually very good for China as an empire during the majority of her ruling years. Under her command, the intellectual class developed greatly, the military enjoyed many enormous successes (especially with the conquering of Korea). Unfortunately, as with many successful leaders of great empires, with age her excesses grew out of control, and corruption and indulgence opened doors to treachery and deceit. By the time she was eighty, the court had turned against her, and murdered the remaining members of her family, as well as her favorite male courtiers. She abdicated in 705, and died a few months later.

Ghengis Khan (1162 - 1227)

There are some leaders in history who achieve greatness and fame through positive actions, through their kindness and wisdom, or their diplomacy. However, there are also those who take the opposite path, and forge their way through time with the point of a sword, spilling blood everywhere they go. Such leaders are fascinating from a historical perspective, as empires formed through death and battle are generally headed by leaders of great charisma and personality – loved and revered by those whose lives they improved and whose borders they expanded, despised and feared by everyone else. History is full of such leaders – some of them simply insane, others callous and ambitious, others misunderstood and misrepresented. However, one particular warlord is still discussed worldwide for the scope of his ambition, and for the sheer numbers he slaughtered. Ghengis Khan, one of the most bloodthirsty and vicious leaders the world ever saw, had a dramatic impact which was felt in almost every corner of the earth, and continues to do so today. What drove him in his attempt to conquer all he saw? Was he a madman, or a military genius? Such questions may never be satisfactorily answered, but the story of this man is utterly compelling in its strangeness and epic content.

If we need some clues as to why Ghengis Khan became the formidable and ruthless leader he was, we can simply look to his childhood for the answer. Mongolia in the 12th century was a difficult part of the world to be born in, plunged as it was in the constant chaos of warfare between the disarrayed and vicious tribes which populated the region. Each tribe had its own agenda, its own ideology and set of beliefs, and the culture of the time dictated that the majority of disputes over family matters, the spread of resources and power had to be solved violently and through battle. As such, the rate of infant mortality was extremely high, and the average lifespan was short and miserable. Ghengis Khan himself was born in the year 1165, to the son of the leader of the Yakka Mongols. However, his life was quickly thrown into turmoil, as at the age of ten, his father was poisoned by a rival and died a painful and gruesome death. As Ghengis Khan, then named Temujin, was the only male heir, he ascended to his father's seat of power and became ruler of the Yakka. The tribe was appalled that they were to be ruled by a mere child, and claimed that they would be humiliated by their enemies and more vulnerable to attack. After all, how could a small child lead them into battle, or negotiate their claims to territory? They quickly plotted to rise up against him, and abandoned him alone in the wilderness before moving on and settling elsewhere with a new leader. Any normal child would have quickly perished in the harsh Mongolian plains, without food or water provided for them, but Temujin was no normal child. He had been raised to be quick-witted and fearless, and survived by scavenging for food, and by hunting and stealing. Before long, he was keeping sheep, and making valuable contacts with other travellers and nomadic peoples.

Just a couple of years later, he had gathered together his own army of dedicated and loyal soldiers. Everyone was amazed by his ruthlessness, his stamina and hunger for power, and before long, people from other tribes were coming to him to serve, so powerful had his reputation become. There is no doubt that Ghengis Khan was a formidable tactician from a young age, and his ambitious nature and murderous activities meant that before long he had taken control of other tribes, frightened them into submission, and had taken control of Mongolia, proclaiming himself leader of the country and the man who would forge them their own empire.

Khan's sights were set on conquering China, a vast country in the 12th century as it is today, and home to a powerful army equipped with the most sophisticated weaponry of the age. However, they had never encountered anything like Khan's hordes – an unstoppable battalion of bloodthirsty Mongols, who would stop at nothing to get what they wanted. Ghengis Khan himself would ride into each city in turn, beheading anyone who raised a weapon to him. His reputation was that of a god, mightily strong and completely fearless, his eyes set only on the prize of conquering the known world. To say he was a megalomaniac would be quite an understatement; he didn't simply want to take over the lands he rode into, he wanted to wash their streets with blood and murder every single citizen who walked them. The mighty Xi Xia and Qin Empires of China fell quickly, with hundreds of thousands of soldiers and civilians dying at the hands of Khan and his tribe. Ghengis Khan wasn't content to simply conquer China, though, and he stretched his empire from the Caspian Sea in the west, to the seas of Japan in the east within a few years, making his the largest empire the world had or has ever seen.

The number of deaths attributed to Ghengis Khan are unparalleled by any other ruler in history. Legend claims that he personally murdered over a million men within one hour, and whilst this cannot be true, the fact that this story is told gives some idea to the extent of his bloodlust. What is true, however, is the fact that he and his men wiped out every citizen of certain cities in very short times indeed, with examples such as the massacre of Nishapur in Persia – where every man, woman and child was killed as an act of vengeance for the death of his son in law. The rest of Khan's life was spent in such a way, killing and plundering cities, leaving very little behind, and spreading the Mongolian people across all of Asia. He died from a riding accident in 1227, but had seen the entire world, and its people, transform within his lifetime. Indeed, Ghengis Khan bedded and raped so many women, in so many different countries, that an astonishing proportion of today's global population would be able to trace their ancestry back to him directly.

Attila The Hun (406AD – 453AD)

Everyone knows that the Roman Empire, even in their later, Christian form, was truly a force to be reckoned with. Their armies of thousands, their perfection of military tactics, their dedication, scope and vision ensured that within a few hundred years, they had conquered the known world, and shaped it for millennia to come. However, despite their might, despite their era of bloodshed and brilliance, there was one leader who filled them with fear, and who forced them into submission, ensuring their later downfall and humiliation. Attila the Hun is one of the classic villains of history, immortalized in records, poetry, plays and paintings – and yet he is a historical figure which many people today know relatively little about. Mention his name, and people will recognize it. They will know that he was tyrant, that he was powerful and feared. Ask for more detail, and the majority will falter and fail to supply it. So, who was the real Attila the Hun? Why did he make one of the great empires of history tremble in their boots? And why do we know so little about him?

Attila the Hun was born in 406 AD, in what is

now modern Hungary. However, as Hungary was only founded approximately a thousand years ago by the nomadic Magyar tribesmen, the people who had settled in this region during Attila's time were a different people – a relatively ragtag brigade of different tribes from the Eurasian Steppes, outcasts from greater Russian civilizations, each with their own laws, traditions and rules. These groups of tribesmen and women were the antithesis of their great enemies, the Romans; they survived through raids and pillage, they lived unordered lives under tribal leaders, who in turn served a king. Despite this, these separate tribes were powerful indeed when united by a common cause or enemy, and their ruthlessness in battle, and almost demonic energy and viciousness meant their reputation spread far and wide. Attila himself was the nephew of King Ruga of the Huns, and when the old King died, Attila succeeded to the throne, to rule alongside his brother Bleda.

Attila, unlike his predecessor, had big plans for his people. He knew that in comparison to the

Romans, or civilizations further east and west of his land, the Huns were nothing – just a marauding group of people, happily carrying out the occasional raid. At some point in his teenage years, Attila's megalomania began to take hold. He decided to start an empire of his own, and leave a trail of blood all along the banks of the mighty Danube river. His first move was an audacious one; to build an army, and take advantage of the now peaceful regions of central Europe long ago left to their own devices by the Romans, but which were still very much a part of the expansive Roman Empire. After sacking and pillaging their way through central Europe, they battled the Roman army themselves, and made quite an impression on the fleeing soldiers, who ran back to the Eastern Roman Empire's capital of Constantinople. There, they told of a terrifying warlord, Attila, and his ambitions to conquer the Balkans and eventually launch an attack on Italy and Turkey. The Emperor, Theodosius II, tried to pacify Attila and his men by offering a hefty tribute in order to avoid further combat. This was accepted, but Attila's thirst for blood and power led him to invade every city within his reach, although they suffered a crippling defeat in Armenia, forcing them to retreat home.

Attila's brother, Bleda, died in a hunting accident in 445 AD, although quite how 'accidental' this event was is open to interpretation. At this point, Attila was sole King of the Huns, and unlike his brother, he was keen to try new techniques and methods for making his mark on history. Attila began to recruit warriors and mobilize his armies, but instead of simply sacking the cities and regions he came across before moving on, he took control of them instead. At this point, the Hun Empire began to be formed, and Attila murdered and massacred his way across Europe, leaving Huns in charge of every town he plundered. With the help of modern siege weapons, Attila had transformed the Huns from wandering marauders to an elite, unified fighting force, and both Rome and Constantinople were deeply afraid. They had come across barbarian tribes before, and had defeated them in battle, but never had they had to face such an organized and utterly vicious army, with no sense of slowing down, or negotiation. They tripled their tribute, and began strengthening the walls of the city of Constantinople in anticipation of an attack. The Romans' fear of the Huns became truly obvious when they sought the help of Celt and Franks, and even made an alliance with their ancient enemy, the Visigoths, in order to defend themselves against this new and ambitious leader. Meanwhile, Attila started his full invasion of the Eastern Roman Empire, and sacked, burned and conquered cities all the way to Greece, now in possession of most of southern Europe and the head of an empire large, strong and powerful enough to equal that of his enemy. The number of heads Attila's army took were countless in number, and torture, rape and mutilation were encouraged as a part of his program to take over Europe as a whole.

Attila's end was a curious one. At the height of his powers, following a string of successful campaigns, he was invited for talks and negotiations by a desperate and frightened Pope

Leo I, who could see his Christian empire being dismantled by a pagan monster of epic ambition and strength. Nobody really knows what happened during these negotiations, but following them, just as the Huns were primed to take over the Romans completely, Attila ordered his army to retreat and return to their homeland. He died soon after from a nosebleed on his wedding day, and without him, his hordes returned to their barbaric state, and his empire collapsed under in-fighting, corruption and a lack of direction.

Ivan the Terrible (1554 - 1581)

Throughout history, empires have risen and fallen at the hands of benevolent geniuses, great and visionary rulers, and those who wish for the success and prosperity of their people. However, at some point in the life cycle of a civilization, the powers bestowed upon an all-powerful ruler will lead to utter corruption, and with the right mixture of violence, megalomania and derangement (helped along, often by a dose of ancestral incest and inbreeding), sheer evil arises. When we think of corrupt and insane rulers and dictators, one particular country is quick to spring to mind: Russia. This vast land, stretching between Europe and the far east, has seen more than its fair share of lunatics in seats of unimaginable power and influence, and as such the entire history of the country is a blood-soaked one. A thousand years ago, the country was divided between dozens of warring factions – tribes with their own ideologies, beliefs and identities, many of which went on to settle around the world after conquering and pillaging other countries. Even in more recent history, Russian leaders have terrified the world with the power they wielded and abused. However, there is one name in Russian history which stands out for the deeds he committed; that of Ivan The Terrible.

Ivan The Terrible was, of course, not always known by this name. He was born in the summer of 1530, the only son of Vasily III, a relatively popular Tsar of Moscow who had been struggling for decades to produce a male heir to his kingdom. Due to the fact that he was old when baby Ivan was born, Vasily died just three years later, partly from old age, and partly due to the fact that he suffered from several inherited health complaints, caused by his weakened bloodline. His death – and the young age of his heir – caused chaos within the palaces, and the three-year-old Ivan was crowned prince of Moscow, having to spend his early childhood in courts and as a presence at hundreds of meetings and political arguments. During this time, Ivan's mother was technically in charge of her late husband's empire, but she too was infirm, and was constantly harangued and bullied by her advisers and the various counts and nobles who were thirsty for power. Just five years after the death of her husband, Ivan's mother succumbed to illness and passed away. Ivan was left as an orphan prince at the age of eight, and he had to watch as all of his parents' work was undone by selfish and power-hungry politicians ruling in their place. There is no doubt about the fact that Ivan's childhood was an exceptionally miserable one. There are many reports and writings – some made by Ivan himself – regarding the vicious treatment he received at the palace as a young prince. He was bullied, beaten and humiliated by those his mother had left to care for him, and despite the fact he was adored by the public, he was deeply neglected in his home, thus spawning a fiery hatred within his young mind towards the ruling classes.

Ivan didn't have to wait too long, however, before he had some real power of his own. When he turned sixteen, he took the title of Tsar of Russia – and made history by being the first man to hold rulership over the whole country. Ivan's first few years as ruler were fascinating to many, and most would be surprised by the fact that at the beginning, it looked as though he would turn out to be a fine ruler, building on the most positive aspects of his father's time as Tsar. Ivan was well educated, and wanted his people to raise their intellectual game. As such, he greatly encouraged the use of the new printing press across Russia, ensuring that books were printed and distributed to his subjects in the east and the west. Furthermore, he enjoyed plenty of military successes in the early years; defeating the troublesome Tatar hordes who had been at war with Moscow for generations. This victory brought with it the first real signs of Ivan's megalomania and capacity for cruelty, though. Not only was the campaign a particularly vicious and bloody one, but it was celebrated with the building of St. Basil's Cathedral – a triumph of architecture that Ivan loved so much that he had the architects' eyes plucked out, to ensure they could never again construct such a wonder.

As Ivan approached middle age, it became dramatically clear that he was not going to be a good ruler after all. In 1553, he suffered a near-fatal illness, and this prompted a dramatic change in his character and policies. He grew increasingly paranoid and suspicious of his staff, and when his wife died of natural causes, he erupted in a fit of rage of madness, accusing several of his noblemen of poisoning her. He then fled from Moscow, leaving behind notes expressing his intention to abdicate. Many people pursued him, and convinced him to return, fearful of the fact that Russia in this time would crumble and collapse in the absence of a strong Tsar. He agreed to return to his throne, but made clear that he would do so as long as he could change the laws and rule as he wished. His nobles agreed, although it was a decision they would soon come to regret.

Ivan's first move when he came back to Moscow was to begin setting up an elite force of secret police, named the Oprichnik. These policemen would have the power to interrogate, torture and murder anyone who displeased Ivan, or anyone who he felt could not be trusted. Of course, the result of this new system was an appalling string of murders which blazed through the country. Within a couple of years, there was not a single family of noble birth who had not had a member killed by this vicious force. Things came to a head in 1570, when Ivan himself rode at the front of a full-on invasion by the Oprichnik of the city of Novgorod, which was razed to the ground and saw the death of thousands of innocent people. In his personal life, Ivan was becoming more and more deranged. He swung between moments of pious, religious devotion and fits of utter madness and rage. He murdered his own son (the groomed heir of the Tsar's throne, no less) indulged in lavish orgies, and killed as he pleased while his great country fell to ruin. His love life also went off the rails, as he married woman after woman, expelling each one to a convent after just a couple of months. Naturally, before long, his people had had more than enough of this lunatic, and it seems likely that he died of mercury poisoning 1584.

Tamerlane the Great (1336 - 1405)

No part of the planet has experienced such glorious highs, such golden ages, followed by periods of crushing poverty and desperation as central Asia. Today, much of the world's news is based around the social and political difficulties of this vast swathe of land, stretching between Turkey in the west, and India and China in the far east, and throughout history, turmoil has been something of a constant. The area south of Russia, where we find modern Georgia, Uzbekistan, Iran and Mongolia, has for a thousand years been fought over, conquered, vanquished, razed and rebuilt, and has given us many of the most powerful, most charismatic, most terrible and terrifying leaders the world has ever known. Surely one of the most formidable, one of the cruelest, most murderous and yet ambitious and successful was the mighty King Tamerlane the Great, conqueror of much of the known world, and terror of Asia. While Tamerlane is perhaps not as well known today as many other rulers, there was a time when he was one of the most famous men in the world, adored by some, feared and despised by most. What cannot be doubted about this controversial ruler, though, is that he changed history – and the fate of many, many countries – forever, and soaked the continent of Asia in the blood of millions.

The man who eventually became known and feared as Tamerlane was born with the name Timur, in the Uzbekistan city of Kesh in the early 14th century. He grew up idolizing the mighty Ghengiz Khan, who he saw as a great liberator, a fiercesome warrior and unparalleled tactician, and decided as a young man that it was his destiny to follow in his footsteps. Despite his complete worship of the great Khan, Timur also felt strongly that his hero never completed what he set out to do, and believed that his fate was to complete the 'unfinished business' started by the Mongol warlords in the generations before his birth. In fact, Timur was so obsessed with associating himself with Ghengiz Khan, he manipulated, murdered and cheated his way up through the ranks of his people, and arranged marriages between himself and the descendants of Ghengiz Khan, to ensure that his own descendants would share both his, and his hero's bloodlines. Early in his military career, it is said that Timur became badly wounded (and archaeological findings support this) in his leg, and he spent all of his adult life with a severe limp. As such, he quickly earned the less-than-glorious title of Tamerlane, or 'Timur The Lame'.

He quickly rose to a position of power within the army of what is now Uzbekistan, and was granted the title of general once his peers and superiors recognized his insatiably appetite for blood and destruction. Sources of the time claim that Tamerlane was a ferocious fighter, and reveled in the chaos of battle. Indeed, before long, whole armies and towns were surrendering the moment they realized who was heading their opponents, so powerful was this young man's reputation and ambition. Before long, under Tamerlane, whole regions of southern Russia were conquered, and most of the Volga basin and the realms around the Caspian Sea were his, before his attentions moved to Iraq, Azerbaijan and more or less the entire length of the silk road. What is surprising about Tamerlane's movements during this early period of his life is that he seemed to care nothing about the people who populated these places – he considered himself nothing less than the new Ghengiz Khan, and yet he slaughtered millions of Mongols in the lands he conquered, Mongols who were descended from Khan's own invading army.

Almost all of central Asia became part of the Timurid empire under Tamerlane's bloodthirsty campaign for dominance. It wasn't long before he decided to ride further east, and continue on a megalomaniacal mission to truly leave his mark on history. At this time, in the mid-14th century, what is now India was experiencing a golden age of its own, but one which was notable for the peacefulness of its politics, and the surprising kindness of its rulers. Tamerlane used all of his evil and cunning to trick to Indian kings into welcoming him into their country, and he headed straight for the capital of Delhi to bring more chaos than the country had ever seen before. The leaders of ancient India quickly assembled an army of sixty battle elephants – a terrifying sight for any invading force, but Tamerlane knew no fear. He gathered hundreds of camels, set them on fire, and sent them galloping towards the Indian army, who scattered along with their elephant cavalry. In a matter of days, 100,000 Indian civilians had been slaughtered in horrendous ways, and India was his for the taking. Indeed, Tamerlane founded the Moghul empire, which reigned in much of India for hundreds of years, and shaped the fate of the country. Bizarrely enough, while he was ravaging Asia, Tamerlane was providing something of a service to the Christian west. The Ottoman's were waging war with much of Europe at the same time as Tamerlane was weaving his destructive path through the east, causing all manner of chaos and distraction, which may well have saved many European countries from Turkish rule at the time.

With India, Persia, Turkey and almost all of central Asia under his control, Tamerlane had turned a continent red with blood. As he reached his sixties, he decided it was time to do what Ghengiz Khan had never managed; take control of China, probably the most powerful and impenetrable country in the world. However, his ambitions were never realized, as he died during the long ride east, after many years of scheming and planning just how this impossible feat would be undertaken.

Caligula (12 - 41 A.D.)

The most famous insane rulers in history have movies made about them. Take the classic trash piece starring Malcolm McDowell, a 1979 Italian-American erotic biographical film that was the first film in history to feature both renowned actors and pornographic scenes, and became one of the leading cult films of all time. Of course, much of the movie is purely fictional, but the screenwriters certainly had a wealth of information to draw from. Contemporary chronicles describe a hedonistic ruler only concerned with luxury and vice, especially sex, and an insane tyrant cruel enough to murder people for his own amusement, all at the expense of the Empire. And, according to Roman historian Suetonius, he did promise to make his horse Inciatus a Roman consul - though he actually invested him as a priest.

Although Caligula reigned for only four years, his egomania and deplorable actions shocked the Roman people. It is little surprise he was the first Roman emperor to be assassinated.

During his father Germanicus' campaign against the Gauls, his three-year-old son Gaius was something like a mascot for the regiment. He donned a miniature infantryman uniform, complete with boots and armor, and swung around a little toy sword. He was so beloved that the regiment nicknamed him Caligula, Latin for "little solider's boots." He was a spoiled, petted child, but nevertheless a charming child the soldiers and his father doted upon.

In 14 A.D., Emperor August - Caligula's paternal grandfather - died; Tiberius was his obvious heir, but the new emperor felt the popular Germanicus was a rival, and according to Suetonius, had him poisoned. Young Caligula was sent to live with his grandmother, Livia, a politically shrewd woman who meddled in her family affairs until her death, after which

Caligula was a prisoner of Tiberius. His brothers were either imprisoned or died of starvation, and it could be this era of terror effected Caligula deeply for the rest of his life.

In 31 A.D., Emperor Tiberius sent him to live on the island of Capri for six years. The remainder of his immediate family was exiled, and died. Caligula was clever enough to stay below the radar so he, too, would not be considered treasonous. Tacitus and Suetonius say of him, "Never was there a better servant or a worse master!"

After Tiberius' shady death in 37 A.D. Caligula and the late emperor's grandson, Gemellus, ruled as joint heirs. The Roman people welcomed him as Germanicus' son and even the chronicler Philo writes the first seven months of his reign were happy ones.

It was when Caligula fell ill in October of that year that his perversions took hold. The first bloody act was adopting his cousin and co-ruler, Gemellus, and then executing him. After his favorite sister, Julia Drusilla, died in 38 A.D., he exiled and likely killed, via poison, the majority of his family.

Clearly, Emperor Caligula had insecurities that forced him to act out in egomaniacal ways. A soothsayer of Tiberius predicted Caligula had "no more chance of becoming emperor than of riding across the Bay of Baiae." In defiance, he built a floating bridge across Baiae and riding his favorite horse, Incitatus, across it wearing the dazzling breastplate of Alexander the Great. Seneca the Younger claimed he did this deliberately to waste money, although the treasury was already in trouble because of recent famines and wars.

Roman Emperors were to an extent worshipped as divine after they were dead, but Caligula took things to a new level when he started appearing in public costumed as various gods and demigods. He presented himself as a god at the sacred Temple of Castor and Pollux on the Forum and even began referring to himself as the Roman god Jupiter, the king of the gods. Caligula's policy of having Romans refer to him as a physical living god was sacrilegious to the extreme.

He alienated the Senate around 39 A.D., when he examined Tiberius' records and decided many of the senators were untrustworthy. Treason trials commenced, and several senators were put to death. The others, degraded.

Chroniclers capture many of his other vicious acts. Seneca the Younger claimed Caligula killed people for his own amusement and openly seduced the wives of enemies (and even the chance friend) and bragged about it to anyone who would listen. Cassius Dio and Suetonius claimed he prostituted his own sisters, and had an incestuous love affair with his favorite, Julia Drusilla, ordered regiments on nonsensical military exercises and turned the Imperial palace into a brothel, where all manners of vice were satiated.

Conspiracies marked the three tyrannical years of his reign, though they were not brought to fruition. The final plot ended his life. In January 41 A.D., the Praetorian Guard attacked Caligula while he addressed a group of actors during the Augustan Games. The leader, Chaerea, whom Caligula mercilessly teased, was the first to stab him. He was stabbed twenty-nine times more.

Even after his death, the madness did not end. Assassins murdered Caligula's wife, Caesonia, and smashed his young daughter's head against a wall. Claudius, his uncle who became emperor after his death, was spared because he had been notified and was in hiding during the assassination. A guardsman found Claudius behind a sheet and declared him emperor of Rome.

To modern readers, it seems Caligula suffered - and had an acute fear - of seizures. Suetonius wrote he suffered from "falling sickness." Other modern readers think Caligula suffered from hyperthyroidism, a condition associated with his eerie stare and some of his worse personality traits: irritability, anger, arrogance and irrationality. Regardless of his diagnosis, Caligula's actions are certainly those of an insane man.

Al-Hakim bi Amr al-Lah (985 - 1021 A.D.)

At best, the "Mad Caliph" al-Hakim bi Amr al-Lah is remembered as an eccentric ruler of one of the most culturally enlightened empires of the medieval world. At worst, a violent madman, religious leader of two different religions and the destroyer of the Holy Sepulcher. The odd reforms is forced on his subjects and murderous cruelty imparted so much fear in his people that no one dared oppose him. That, and his divine right to rule led true believers, who although confused and fearful of his actions, to continue their abiding devotion until his death. In short, the rulc of al-Hakim is a strong argument against the divine right of kings, a concept perfected in the Middle Ages and spanning the Western and Muslim world.

Al-Hakim was born in 985 to one of the two consorts of Caliph al-'Aziz, the supreme ruler of the Fatimid Empire - or Caliphate. The Fatimids were descendants of Prophet Muhammad's daughter, and belonged to the

Islamic Isma'ili Shi'a sect of faith that flourished as a political power with the Fatimid Empire between the tenth and twelfth centuries. At the height of its power, the Fatimid Caliphate spanned Palestine, Syria, North Africa and its Red Sea coast, Yemen, the Tihamah and Hejaz. It included holy Mecca, Jerusalem, Tripoli, Alexandria, its capitol Cairo, Palermo and Fez, cities important to the trade routes that flourished under Fatimid rule.

At 11, al-Hakim ascended as ruler of the empire, although it was as a figurehead. Three years later his reckless reign really began. He faced growing opposition from the Abassid Caliphate in Baghdad that practiced Sunni Islam and therefore tried to stop the influence of the Fatimid's Shi'a practices. There was also unrest within the military between Turks and Berber factions, and tension between al-Hakim and his viziers, or advisers, concerning the rise of a religious sect that formed around the caliph and regarded him as a manifestation of God.

Religious tensions defined the era, and al-Hakim's attitude toward religion was highly problematic. He was hostile to nearly every religion save his own. Between 996 and 1006, he began his strange reforms against other religions. He attacked Sunni Muslims first by posting public cursing against the first three caliphs (Abu Bakr, Umar and Uthman ibn Affan), and forbade certain morning prayers because he felt they were *too* Sunni.

Next he attacked the Christian and Jewish faiths by ordering them to wear discriminatory clothing - a black belt and turban. Additionally, Christians were forced to wear an iron cross and Jews had to wear a wooden calf necklace. When they used public baths, Jews had to replace the calf necklace with a bell. Christian and Jewish women were forced to wear shoes of two different colors, one black and one red. In 1003, he ordered a church destroyed and replaced with an Islamic mosque. Just as problematic, in 1004 he decreed that Christians could not practice Epiphany or Easter services, and forbade Christians and Jews from imbibing drinks made from grapes, meaning Christians could no longer use wine during their communion rites and Jews could no longer use it during their festivals.

He created restrictive ordinances for women, such as forbidding women to appear in public with their faces covered.

Al-Hakim's irrational hatred of Christians culminated in 1009, when he destroyed the Holy Sepulcher and associated buildings. This angered Christian bishops and princes of kingdoms that would later cite the destruction of his holy monument as a catalyst for the First Crusade in 1096 and subsequent crusades afterward. He prohibited Christian processions like the Descent of the Holy Fire, and within a few years all of the churches and convents in

Palestine had been confiscated or even destroyed.

Other strange tyrannies abounded. He routinely killed viziers every few years, and replaced them with new ones. After he sacked al-Fustat near Cairo, he killed all of the dogs because their barking annoyed him, and banned certain vegetables and shellfish.

Between 1012 and 1021, al-Hakim's attitude toward Christians and Jews softened, and he even allowed them to rebuild many of their homes and places of worship, although he remained hostile toward Sunni Muslims.

Around 1017, he began distancing himself from the Fatimid's Shi'a faith. An Isma'ili Shi'a student named Muhammed al-Durzi started preaching that al-Hakim, as a descendant of the Prophet, was a manifestation of God, a theological principal similar to Jesus being a manifestation of the Christian God. Many considered this heretical, although al-Hakim did not because there is no evidence, he persecuted this new belief in the slightest, and certainly not with the eccentric fervor he used when persecuting other religions. This belief became central to the new sect, called the Druze faith, which even today has thousands of followers in Syria and Lebanon.

In spite of his erratic acts of tyranny, al-Hakim was a notable patron of the arts and education. In 1005, he founded the Dar al-'ilm, or House of Knowledge, where scholars taught a breadth of subjects, from the Qur'an to astronomy, to any interested member of the public. Many Shi'a missionaries received part of their training from the Dar al-'ilm, which served scholars until the Fatimid dynasty's downfall. During famines, he attempted to stabilize food prices for subjects.

There is no account of how al-Hakim died. At the end of his reign, the Mad Caliph became more ascetic, more secluded. He often took walks during the night. In February of 1021, he went on a night walk after meditating and never returned. He was 36. It remains a likely possibility he was murdered, for a search party found bloodstained clothing and a donkey with no rider. His son Ali az-Zahir succeeded him under the regency of al-Hakim's impressive daughter Sitt al-Mulk.

His divine right to rule was problematic because it allowed him to indulge in tyrannical public ordinances and murder advisors on a whim without being checked by any reasonable power. Those who remained loyal to him as the chosen one, the members of the Druze faith, were persecuted harshly after his disappearance.

Charles VI (1368 - 1422)

King Charles VI reigned during one of France's darkest hours. Amidst the calamitous years of the Black Death, peasant revolts, papal schisms, famine and The Hundred Years' War, he took an active leadership role when he was sane - and when he was not, there was a power vacuum that sparked a blood feud.

It seems likely Charles VI was by modern definition schizophrenic. Contemporary chroniclers such as Jean Froissart and St Denis' chronicler-monk Pintoin mention his violent, emotional outbursts, bizarre delusions and hallucinations triggered by his paranoia. His reactions to imagery and even beloved family members are symptomatic of the kind of breakdown of thought common in people with schizophrenia. The strain appears to have originated from his mother, Queen Joanna of Bourbon's (1338 - 1378), side; she suffered a mental collapse after the birth of her seventh child.

Before the first episode of illness, Charles VI was considered a dazzling sportsman and competent ruler, although chroniclers note he was particularly lustful. Even after the onset of his episodes, courtiers sought a mistress to warm his bed and satisfy his sexual urges.

The first episode occurred in 1393 in Brittany, in which a member of his retinue was attacked by assassins. This triggered the king to take up his sword and thrash wildly about those around him. In his frenzy, he killed four of his knights. From that moment, he developed delusions that he was being pursued by enemy assassins wherever he went.

Beginning in 1395, the king began experiencing psychotic periods that plagued him for the rest of his life. He began insisting he was not named Charles, that he was not king. He rejected hygiene; he refused to bathe, to shave, to change his soiled linen or clothing, or to eat or sleep at normal hours. His body was covered in boils. He exhausted himself running through the corridors of the Hôtel Saint-Pol, his royal townhouse in Paris. He did not recognize courtiers, his children or his wife and queen, Isabeau of Bavaria, and in his madness, attacked her as well as anything emblazoned with her coat of arms. One medieval chronicler mentioned him making obscene gestures and even urinating on her banner. After the disastrous defeat at the Battle of Agincourt in 1415, Charles scandalized everyone by holding a tournament eight months later.

When Charles experienced periods of sanity, frivolity abounded. His court was filled with astrologers, magicians and moneylenders. Mystery plays and decadent and extreme fashions flourished. Queen Isabeau and the Duchess of Orléans often competed with each other using sumptuous gowns and fantastical headpieces. In one horrifying incident of courtly spectacle, later named *Bal des Ardents*, six men, including the king, dressed up as wood savages for a wedding ceremony. Their costumes were made of linen cloth and soaked in pitch - an extremely flammable substance - so torches were not permitted. However, the Duke of Orléans entered the chamber with a torch as the savages entertained, a spark fell and ignited the monsters one by one. The young Duchess de Berry recognized the king in disguise and with her skirt smothered the flames, yet four lords died, some by suffocation, fire or ghastly wounds sustained from the incident. This occurred just months after Charles VI's first psychotic episode, and surely heightened his illness.

Even before Charles VI was anointed king, the French realm was dismal: the coffers were exhausted, the Great Pestilence still emerged every decade or so and the Hundred Years' War with England was going badly. Charles VI's lunacy only contributed to this miserable period.

Because of his inability to rule during his periods of insanity, the peers of the realm established a regency to rule in his stead. Headed by Queen Isabeau and the Princes of the Blood who allied themselves in different ways to accommodate their political aims, the regency was almost as unstable as its king. The king's brother, Louis the Duke of Orléans, and the king's cousin Jean the Duke of Burgundy fought and schemed for control of the throne until 1407, when Burgundy's hired assassin killed Orléans in the streets of Paris. This plunged Francc into a blood feud known as the Armagnac-Burgundian Civil War (1407 - 1435), which tore the kingdom apart and left it weakened for the English King Henry V and his remarkable victory at Agincourt, where he plucked the last great French flower of chivalry.

Reactions to mental illness in the High Middle Ages varied. Mentally ill people were both feared and pitied. Friends and family brought them to shrines for cures, but they almost always kept them chained or guarded. Physicians recommended sleep, bleeding, ointments, potions, baths and happiness. They also warned against sorcery and, in this particularly miserable time, demons.

King Charles VI had strong reactions to imagery, although some of them were positive. One piece of art from his reign and in response to his madness was his secretary Pierre Salmon's lovely *Dialogues*, a collection of illuminated manuscripts, known as a Mirror of Princes, aimed at humbly counseling the king. Many of the pages are gorgeous pictorial renderings of advice, theological questions and ethical situations aimed to make a visual impact on the mad king. Another piece of art dated from his reign were tarot cards, or playing cards. Modern historians attribute his mistress, Odette de Champdivers, introducing them to the French court to keep the king entertained. She was less of a lover, although she did produce one illegitimate child with the mad king, and more of a nursemaid who soothed Charles during his fits of insanity. According to a chronicler, his last thoughts before his death concerned her wellbeing.

At the time of his death in 1422, the debilitating Treaty of Troyes had been signed, giving Henry V huge power of the French realm, the blood feud between Armagnacs and Burgundians was still bloodying the countryside and there were still two popes, one in French Avignon. His son succceded him as Charles VII. He did not exhibit symptoms like his father, but his grandson, the English king Henry VI (1421 - 1417) seems to have suffered from a similar mania.

Charles VI is nicknamed "the Mad" but also "the Beloved," a testament to some of the medieval attitudes about mental illness. Not a cruel tyrant like the Roman Emperor Caligula, the French king was more of a tragic figure burdened with mental instability in a dire, dark time of his kingdom's history.

Erik XIV (1533 - 1577)

When this insane king of Sweden was young, he proposed marriage to Princess Elizabeth Tudor, later Queen Elizabeth I, against his father's wishes. After being turned down by the woman later referred to as the "Virgin Queen," he made other unsuccessful marriage proposals to noblewomen across Europe, including Mary, Queen of Scots, Anne of Saxony, Renata of Lorraine and Christine of Hesse. In hindsight, they were probably counting their lucky stars for rejecting the young Swedish prince. He wasn't the type of monarch above imprisoning noble families on a whim, or stabbing prisoners himself.

Observing a sixteenth century painting of him, he appears every inch a handsome nobleman of the Renaissance. Indeed, he was an authentic Renaissance prince; Erik and his half-brother received a typical nobleman's Renaissance education from a well-versed tutor or group of tutors who taught them history, political thought and geography. He took an interest in aesthetic values, astrology, culture and military science. He was also gifted with special talents in languages, mathematics composition, especially histories, and the playing the lute. He was a splendid rider, swimmer and dancer.

Erik was born Erik Wasa at the royal castle in Stockholm. He was the eldest son of Gustav I, who was born a nobleman but led the fight for Swedish independence. Gustav was crowned King of Sweden in 1523. Politically, he was extremely shrewd and able, but he had his dark behaviors as well. Many of his actions that troubled Erik's childhood were symptomatic of Erik's own violent personality, suggesting his mental illness was hereditary. For example, Gustav attacked a goldsmith who had taken a day off from work without his permission. The goldsmith died of his injuries. Dagger in hand, he chased around the palace courtyard a secretary who irritated him. His violence did not halt for his family. During one outburst, his daughter Cecile upset him, so he tore out her hair. The end of his reign was marked by senility. Despite his violent outbursts and suspicious nature, he is still regarded as a great Swedish king.

His father appointed Erik as acting Regent between 1555 and 1556 during his Russian campaign. A year later, he made him Duke of Kalmar, a collection of provinces that included a permanent residence for the prince. Gustav I loathed the company Duke Erik kept at his Kalmar estate, and referred to them as a "group of toads." In reality, they weren't all bad; the group was composed of artistic, well-educated young men from rustic backgrounds who lived in decadence with the young duke. Erik was fond of good food and drink, music, art, sex and fabulous clothing. Unfortunately, he also drank excessively, and to the horror of his father, he and his "group of toads" conducted orgies at his

Kalmar residence.

Erik succeeded his father to the Swedish throne on September 29, 1560. His coronation was an elaborate display of royal power, and Erik became the first Swedish monarch to style himself "His Majesty." A product of the Renaissance, he updated the royal castle with modern stucco, filigree inlaid woods and tapestries from the masters in Flanders.

Although his father had been content ruling an independent Swedish state, Erik wanted to expand Sweden's influence into the Baltic. This goal put him at odds with the nobility, including his younger half-brother John, who at the time was the Duke of Finland, later King John III of Sweden. In 1562, Duke John defied his Erik by marrying Princess Catherine Jagiellona of Poland, making him on friendly terms with one of the countries Erik wanted to conquer, and invading Livonia. Erik ordered him seized and tried for high treason. He was imprisoned, waiting in dread for Erik's decision regarding his life. Erik ordered John's loyal servants to be executed, but in the end, he released his half-brother. They embraced one another with tears in their eyes.

The period between 1563 and 1570 was marked by King Erik's attempt to dominate the Baltic region and Estonia, furthering Swedish power. This "Nordic Seven Years' War" resulted in great brutality against the civilian populations of Denmark and Poland. Erik occasionally led military ventures, although he spent the majority of the Nordic Seven Years' War as a desk-commander in the presence of his advisors and "group of toads."

As his mania became more pronounced - alternating between violent outbursts and sorrowful repentance - he began acting like his father. He sentenced two guards to death for annoying him. Suspicious that another Swedish nobleman would overthrow him, he assumed any sound made at the wrong time, like the clearing of one's throat, was a sign of plotting against him. He even executed handsome pages and servants, on the charge that they were seducing the noble ladies of his court.

The most infamous incident of his reign is remembered by Swedes today. By 1567, his mental illness was obvious. It is likely he was schizophrenic, evidenced by his dramatic mood swings and paranoia. His suspiciousness led him to arrest and convict several aristocrats, particularly the influential Sture family, of high treason. Two members, Nils Sture and his father Svante Sture, were held in Uppsala Castle, where he visited under the guise of reconciling with the noblemen. Instead, he himself stabbed Nils Sture. Then he ordered the guards to murder the other prisoners, and fled on horseback. Even when his loyal tutor followed him to calm him down, Erik stabbed him as well.

As with the pattern of his mental illness, his violent outburst was followed by a period of guilt and repentance. He secluded himself in Svartsjö Castle, just outside of Stockholm, for several months.

In 1568, the noblemen finally acted to curb Erik's tyranny. They forced him to abdicate the throne, replacing him with his brother John III, and imprisoned him within various castles over the next few years. In 1577, he died at Örbyhus Castle of arsenic poisoning. Legend has it it was his own brother who ordered the mad king's pea soup poisoned.

King Erik XIV of Sweden was a promising Renaissance prince turned into a violent schizophrenic. His mental illness was likely hereditary; besides his father, his sister Princess Sophia also suffered from their affliction. After years of domestic abuse, Sophia lived secluded at Ekolsund Castle, where she dismissed the head butler 21 times, but there is no evidence she possessed the cruelty capable of either Gustav Wasa or his son, Erik.

Erzsebet Bathory (1560 - 1614)

The "Bloody Countess" is a favorite subject of historical fiction and films. According to popular folklore, Erszebet was something of a vampire, killing young virgins and using their blood to stay young, but even the "factual" history of this Hungarian countess is disturbing. Like Gilles de Rais, she was a historic prolific serial killer - some label her as the most prolific female one in history - although shadowy history leaves the number of victims up for debate.

Erzsebet came from one of the most prominent noble Protestant families in Hungary. She was born on the family estate of Nyirbator in 1560 or 1561, spending her childhood in Nagy-Esced near the Romanian border. Her parents were György Bathory of Esced. Her mother was Anna Bathory, who was a sister to Stephen Bathory, the king of Poland and the prince of Transylvania. Erzsebet had several Transylvanian cousins, a contribution to her reputation as the female Dracula.

Her childhood was far from unhappy, although she had a cruel older brother. Much of it was spent in tranquility in the Esced estate learning to read and write in Hungarian, Latin, German and Greek. She was said to be a ravishing woman with long hair and a clear complexion, voluptuous in figure. Rumors claimed she became pregnant in 1574. She gave birth to a bastard daughter in seclusion, which was apparently spirited away to grow up with the peasant who had impregnated the young noblewoman.

In 1570, when Erzsebet was 11, she was betrothed to Count Ferencz Nadasdy de Nasasd of Fogarasfold, later nicknamed the "Black Hero" for his victories in battle. They married in May of 1575 when she was 16 in front of 4,500 guests. The festivities lasted weeks before the newlyweds moved to Nadasdy Castle in Sarvar; however, Ferenc left to study in Vienna, leaving his young bride to entertain herself. Eight years later, Ferenc, as chief commander, led Hungarian troops to war against the Ottoman Turks. Again, Erzsebet was left to her own devices, this time including fashionable Italian sexy toys and Venetian hair bleach. She spent her time brewing herbal teas, potions, drugs and powders.

Although she was beautiful and nobly born, Erzsebet had a violent temper, which she took out on hapless servants. She did not merely punish them with beatings, but whipped them until they bled, and tortured them with all manner of cruel devices, such as razors and branding irons. Some historians suggest she learned these cruel tricks from her aunt, Klara Bathory of Esced, rumored to be a bisexual torturer who killed her second husband.

Erzsebet gave birth to several children during the 29 years of her marriage to Ferencz. He died in 1604, victim of a battle would or illness caused by battle. During and the Long

War (1593 - 1606) her husband fought, she was the sole manager of his castle. It was during this period that many of her atrocities were committed.

The actual number of victims vary, with some estimates as high as 600. In the end she was convicted of 80 murders.

Folklore claims that after the countess turned 40, she began feeling desperate for some beauty elixir. During a violent outburst, she struck a serving girl so hard she bled. Some of the young girl's blood splattered on the skin of the countess, who remarked how it made her appearance more youthful. To supplement her fading beauty, she allegedly hanged peasant women above her bath, letting their fresh blood trip into the tub and enrich her appearance. When this method failed, she began kidnapping the daughters of nobles. However, this vampiric folklore is pure speculation.

Instead, it seems Erzsebet was something

of a sadist. Beginning in 1600, she paid trusted
serving maids to recruit virgin peasant girls to
serve her. Few peasant families could resist
sending their daughters to such a fortunate life
in the Bathory castle. It was not a fortunate life -
their master stripped, bound, beat and tortured
them until they died. One of her favorite devices
was a long, cylindrical cage made of iron that
hung from the ceiling like a suspended iron
maiden. She placed the young servants in them
and hoisted them up, whereby the spikes
penetrated their skin and they bled out.

Shc wcnt further. When she turned fifty,
she felt the need to torture daughters of the
lesser gentry. She beat, burned, bite and
mutilated them as well.

Rumors spread about the atrocities
committed by Countess Bathory. Because she
was nobly born and well-connected, she was
spared a public trial. In December of 1610,
Palatine Gyorgy Thurzo of Hungary, sent by

King Matthias II of Hungary, arrested the countess and four of her accomplices. The trial began two weeks later, during which dozens of survivors and witnesses testified against the countess. One of her servants also testified against her. The court also examined the grounds of the castle and found cadavers of her victims.

Erzsebet and her four accomplices were found guilty on 80 counts of murder, although eye witnesses testify there were far more victims. The accomplices were tortured and killed.

The countess was never actually brought to trial, but she was permanently imprisoned following it. Her family, disgraced by her demonic actions, were the ones to imprison her, locking her in a small brick set of rooms. They passed food to her through slits. She died four years later in 1614. The villagers protested her original burial near the castle, so her body was moved to the Bathory family crypt at Esced.

The "Bloody Countess" inspired plenty of folk legends and entries in popular culture. The first mention of her bathing in the blood of virgins appears in a 1729 Hungarian story. Later tales attribute her to Transylvanian Dracula vampirism. She remains a notable serial killer, and one of the most infamous historical sadists. It is chilling to imagine what kinds of acts of cruelty she would have performed had she been a queen instead of a mere countess.

Mustafa I (1591 - 1639)

The Ottoman Turks produced a strong dynasty
of great sultans who ruled in a row, leading their
kingdom to glory. The unfortunate Sultan
Mustafa I was not one of them.

The Ottoman Empire lasted eight decades,
from the thirteenth century until 1923. Hordes
of Turkish warriors began migrating over
Anatolia and into Asia Minor during the late
thirteenth century. Their greatest prize was
Constantinople, which they sacked in 1453, to
the horror of Western Christians, and renamed
Istanbul. The Ottoman Empire was purely
dynastic, meaning its territories were determined
by administrative and military power, not
religious, ethnic or cultural partitions. Because
of this, the Ottomans were able to encompass
large swathes of land into its Islamic fold.
Throughout its existence as a world state, the
Empire acquired territories in North Africa, the
Mediterranean, across the Black Sea, into the
Arabian Peninsula, including holy Mecca, and

land surrounding the Red Sea, including Jerusalem, fought over so viciously during the medieval crusades. It ended in 1923 after committing atrocities against the Armenians during the Genocide.

After Sultan Suleiyman the Great's reign, the Ottoman Empire witnessed a decline. His son Selim II was disinterested in ruling, and the empire suffered. However, the empire Mustafa inherited was still the wealthiest and most militaristically powerful state in the seventeenth century world.

After a short reign, Mustafa's older brother Ahmed I died of typhus, and Mustafa succeeded him to the throne in 1617. Fraternal succession in the Empire was a curious practice. The Ottomans believed the Sultan was chosen by divine *kut*, or favor. Therefore, every male member of the royal ruling family was a claimant to the throne. This resulted in succession wars between rival brother claimants. To strengthen their claim, new sultans often ordered the death of their relatives; even infants were not spared. In order to continue the dynasty and prevent fratricide, Ahmed I confined potential claimants instead of murdering them. The practice established *Kafes*, or "The Cage."

Mustafa was confined to *Kafes* for 14 years. *Kafes* existed in the Imperial Harem of the palace, a safe, though isolated, place to keep rivals. Mustafa had access to opium and alcohol. Food was brought to him through a slit in the wall of his small room. According to some accounts, he shared this room with Ahmed before Ahmed was enthroned. Other accounts mention occasional women visitors, although they do not go into detail about Mustafa's dealings with them. After Ahmed's ascent, Mustafa was under constant surveillance, yet very alone. The conditions of his imprisonment in *Kafes* contributed to his already weak mental state. Chroniclers report he was at best neurotic

128

and feebleminded; at worst mentally retarded. Confinement, opiates, alcohol and isolation only made the situation worse.

Because of his weak mind, Mustafa I was no more than a court pawn. The vacuum of power in the Empire due to his inability to rule allowed wasteful spending, general corruption and evil deeds to flourish. In 1618, after mere months, he was deposed and returned to *Kafes*. His young, untried nephew Osman II became Sultan. One of the many problems with the succession practice was that years of imprisonment left potential rulers hardly fit to rule. They were not invested with the kind of experience or education to effectively guide one of the world's greatest empires.

His nephew Osman II had potential for greatness, but he was assassinated four years into his reign. He was 18. He was an accomplished poet and linguist, and brokered peace with Iran, securing the eastern border. Trouble stirred when he blamed the Janissaries, or household guard, for the defeat against Poland. He attacked them by closing their coffee shops, where they conspired to reshape the Turkish military, and in retaliation, the Janissaries and *sipahis*, or cavalry, imprisoned and killed the young monarch in 1622. Patricide was common, but the guards' murder of Osman was the first known regicide in the Ottoman Turk's history.

Inexplicably, Mustafa I once again reigned as Sultan. He ordered the deaths of those involved with his nephew's coup for the throne, although he missed Osman. In his madness, he ran throughout the imperial palace, pounding on doors and weeping for his nephew to take over his burden of kingship.

Mustafa was madder than before. He ordered Ahmed's sons to be executed, but the household guard intervened and instead crowned his oldest son as Murad IV. Mustafa renounced his throne, at the behest of the wise

Grand Mufti, the highest religious authority in the land. Sixteen years later, he died where he was born, in the Topkapi Palace in Istanbul.

Sultan Mustafa I is a rather sad tale of puppet-king burdened by horrendous circumstances. He grew up isolated in a cage, a preventative measure against his claim to the throne, a practice established to deter the unfortunately bloody Ottoman succession policy. He was once again confined there after his nephew's coup. He took no pleasure in ruling one of the greatest empires the world has known. Indeed, even modern historians treat his name as a footnote, his insanity meriting interest, so many details of his personal life are lost in the grand backcloth of the Ottoman Empire's history

George III (1738 - 1820)

Add King George III of England to the list of monarchs mad enough to make a movie about (although "The Madness of King George" was a play before it was a movie). George III's reign was longer than any British king, and third longest behind those of Queen Victoria and Elizabeth II. Nine of those years were troubling ones, for the monarch was incapacitated by blindness, partial deafness and insanity roughly the last decade of his life until his death.

In children's history books, George III is dubbed "the mad king who lost America." Modern historians have attributed his insanity to porphyria, a genetic blood disorder. Aches, pains and blue urine are some of the symptoms. However, recent, ongoing research from St George's at the University of London has confirmed that King George suffered from mental illness. By studying thousands of handwritten letters, researchers found that during his insane episodes, his sentences were far longer than when he was sane. For instance, George often repeated himself, throwing in increasingly creative vocabulary, so a handwritten sentence of 400 words and only eight verbs is hardly unusual; it was symptomatic of his mental illness. Other aspects he displayed, such as mania and convulsions, are attributed to bipolar disorder.

A good example: George III spoke nonsense to himself for 58 hours over Christmas in 1819.

During the last nine years of his reign, Great Britain faced many of the same problems as France in the early 15th century. George III often withdrew to Kew Palace during bouts of mania. While he was secluded, an informal regency was established. The Prince of Wales desired to be appointed regent, but both his father King George and the government refused to support him. In the end, it was the British government that acted on behalf of the king in all but name, not bickering peers of the realm like during Charles VI's reign, because by this time, Britain had a constitutional king.

George III faced numerous obstacles during his reign. The first years were troubled by political instability due to disagreements over the Seven Years' War. The Tory and Whig parties fought for control of the Parliament of England.

The American Revolution and the loss of the American colonies marred George III's reputation. By the end of the war, Britain's coffers were quite empty.

Deeply pious, King George spent hours in prayer. He was appalled by his brothers' loose moral. Prince Henry, the duke of Cumberland and Strathearn, was a known adulterer who married a young widow far below his station as a prince of the realm. This inspired him to pass a law that required his consent for any member of the Royal Family to marry. It was very unpopular.

His appointment of William Pitt as Prime Minister was the opposite, and spoke of his diplomacy in dealing with the public mood and the House of Commons. His popularity increased as the first signs of mental illness appeared in 1765.

Modern hair strand tests attribute his deteriorating health and mental state to a high level of arsenic from medicines or cosmetics coupled with bipolar disorder. After he suffered a brief episode in 1765, a longer episode began in 1788. He went to Cheltenham Spa to revive himself, but his condition still worsened. In November of 1788, he became very deranged. His voice grew hoarse from hours upon hours of talking to himself, worked up into such a frenzy that he foamed at the mouth. Rumors claimed he talked to a tree he mistook as the King of Prussia.

The methods for treating mental illness in

the eighteenth century were hardly different than those of previous centuries. The king's physicians tried forcibly restraining him until he became calm. Foul poultices were used to "draw out the evil," and were ineffective.

Since the ascent of the Hanoverian dynasty, Britain was a constitutional monarchy. Prime Minister Pitt effectively ruled the realm during George III's bouts of illness. Their popularity increased, aided by George III's merciful treatment of two demented assailants, Margaret Nicholson in 1786 and John Firth in 1790, who attempted to physically assault his person.

In winter of 1810, the king became extremely ill. Although he was at the height of his popularity, he was nearly blind with cataracts, suffering from rheumatism and partially deaf. The death of his youngest and dearest daughter, Princess Amelia, triggered even more stress. Aware of his decreasing health, he accepted the Regency Act of 1811, which made the Prince of

Wales Regent of England. The Prince acted as Regent until King George's death.

From 1811 until his death, George lived sequestered in Windsor Castle. His physical and mental health increasingly deteriorated until he was unaware, he was the king of England, or that he wife, Charlotte of Mecklenburg-Strelitz, had died in 1818.

After his death on January 29, 1820, his two sons succeeded him as king, but they did not produce legitimate heirs. Queen Victoria, the last of the House of Hanover, succeeded to the throne after their deaths.

Although he was a victim of mental illness and political turmoil, George III had several accomplishments. The British Agricultural Revolution provided a meaningful outlet for his often-mocked interest in agriculture. Under his rule, rural output increased, as did the populace, contributing to the Industrial Revolution's workforce. As a patron of the arts, George III increased the Royal Academy of Arts' collection by donating large grants from his own private funds. He purchased Johannes Vermeer's *Lady at the Virginals* and a set of Canalettos. He also funded an impressive library - the King's Library, which was open to the scholars. In addition to artistic support, he collected mathematical and scientific instruments. He funded William Herschel's 40-foot telescope project. Herschel discovered Uranus; at first, he named it George's Star after his patron.

While his younger sister Caroline Mathilde was struggling with her own mad king of Denmark, George III of England reigned a long and tumultuous time suffering from mental illness himself. His mental illness seems to be related to bipolar disorder, possibly triggered by arsenic poison and absolutely triggered by stress. Britain was fortunate at that time to be a constitutional monarchy, allowing Prime Minister Pitt to rule on behalf of the insane king, who, compared to other monarchs, spared his subjects much of blood caused by the aimless violence of a diseased mind.

Christian VII (1749 - 1808)

The story of insane king Christian VII of Denmark is really a story of his wicked stepmother, his enlightened court physician and his lonely English wife.

There is no disputing that King Christian was mentally unsound. The realm was ruled by him nominally, actually by a series of royal advisors who struggled or allied based on their goals with Dowager Juliane Marie of Brunswick-Wolfenbuttel, Christian's stepmother. His inability to rule left unchecked the Danish Revolution of the late 1760s and early 1770s, later referred to as the Struensee Era, named for the royal physician, and true ruler of Denmark who ignited it from his desk.

Even as a child, Christian was peculiar. He was born on January 29,1749 at Christianborg Palace in Copenhagen. His father was King Frederick V of Denmark, his mother Princess Louise of Great Britain. After his mother died, King Frederick married the indomitable Juliane

Marie of Brunswick-Wolfenbuttel, who wielded significant power during Christian's reign.

His education was neglected; his governor, Count von Reventlow, believed in absolute discipline and routinely brutalized the poor prince, who was already showing signs of mental imbalance. By some accounts before he was under Reventlow's tutelage, he was a charming and talented young man displaying periods of clarity. All in all, young Christian was a cruel, insecure and poorly educated young man, completely unfit for the Danish throne. As an adult, he was much the same.

His father, Frederick V, died on the morning of January 14, 1766. He was only 42, but the years of alcoholism had taken their toll. Christian was anointed a week before his seventeenth birthday.

Now a divine king, Christian acted how he pleased. He was an eternal child, playing leapfrog, terrorizing brothels and vandalizing shops in Copenhagen. He particularly enjoyed public executions, so much so that he had his courtiers build him his own rack and he played the man marked for death on a few occasions.

The Queen of Denmark had the misfortune of being sister to one mad king, and wife to another. In 1766, the young king of Denmark married Princess Caroline Mathilde, the sister of "Mad King" George III of England. However, George III was considered competent for the majority of his reign, exhibiting no serious signs of mental instability until the last decade or so, while her husband disturbed his family from his childhood onward.

After Christian and Caroline Mathilde married, he abandoned himself to sexual excesses. She, on the other hand, grieved constantly. He had gone as far as to declare it was unfashionable to love wives. Under her mother's protection in Britain, the princess had grown up cloistered. Christian did not allow her to have any of her ladies-in-waiting from home, so she was alone and neglected while her insane husband pursued prostitutes and young men. One in particular became his favorite: the courtesan Støvlet-Catherine (or "Boots-Catherine," as her mother ran a boots shop), a tall, beautiful woman who became his official mistress in 1767. The Queen Dowager, Christian's stepmother, decided she had too much influence at court, and had her arrested, imprisoned and exiled a year later, but she certainly left her mark on the Danish king; he referred to her as the "Mistress of the Universe."

After Boots-Catherine was exiled, King Christian sank into a deep depression, or even a mental stupor. His advisors agreed the only way to relieve him was a tour of Europe. Because of the deterioration of the king's mental state, an upcoming German doctor, Johann Friedrich Struensee, accompanied him on his tour, which was surprisingly successful. Struensee was an intelligent, handsome physician of the Enlightenment. He seemed to be the only man who could manage the strange monarch, and as Christian grew stranger, Struensee became more powerful. By 1769, the German doctor was the "de facto" regent of Denmark while Christian grew worse. He beat his head against walls, mumbled incoherently, attacked and ridiculed his entourage and sat alone for hours in a stupor. He was plagued by hallucinations and paranoia. He struggled with his identity as king; he seemed convinced he was a peasant changeling exchanged at birth, not the true king of Denmark. All of these are symptomatic of schizophrenia.

While King Christian played with his Black servant and dog in an oblivious childhood state, Struensee ran the kingdom. He acted as king in another way as well; in 1769, he visited Queen Caroline Mathilde who had grown fat and depressed. He suggested they go horseback riding to allow her fresh air and exercise. Before long they were lovers. Some historians speculate he used her as a means to obtain more royal power, but others are convinced they were in love. Caroline Mathilde bore him a daughter; her other child was Christian's son, the prince.

Caroline Mathilde was sensual and naive; she spoke openly of her affair with the German physician with her chambermaids. Struensee was already garnering disfavor from council members for his radical reforms. From his desk, he wrote edicts that opened the royal gardens to the public, legalized freedom of speech and abolished torture, unfree labor and other practices he and other Enlightened thinkers considered unjust. One immensely unpopular reform was aimed at abolishing public scorn for single mothers and adulteresses. Between the queen's naivety and Struensee's idealism, they were doomed to fail. The Queen Dowager schemed use their affair to remove them from

Christian's life.

Struensee was tried and executed for high treason; Caroline Mathilde was exiled to Celle Castle in Hannover for life, where she died a few years later. Accounts reveal the king was unaware he signed Struensee's death warrant, and still called for Struensee, who had been his close confidant.

Although Christian ruled Denmark until his death in name, the true rulers were the Queen Dowager, a conservative courtier named Ove Guldberg and Christian's drooling half-brother, Crown Prince Frederick. He died at 59 of a stroke.

Christian VII's mental illness, the Danish Enlightenment and Queen Caroline Mathilde's affair with Struensee have provided the basis for literature, films and plays.

Norton I (1819 - 1880)

The United States has certainly witnessed some rather odd fellows in power, but the looniest by far was the only self-proclaimed ruler during the country's short history. The U.S. has had many presidents, but only one emperor. This was Imperial Majesty Emperor and Protector of Mexico Joshua Abraham Norton I.

Norton was born in England, although sources are unclear about the year. Some report 1815, others 1819. He spent the majority of his early life in South Africa with his parents, John and Sarah Norton, a wealthy Jewish merchant's sister. In 1849, he arrived in San Francisco after being given a bequest of $40,000 from his father's estate. He arrived on a fanciful-sounding steam batch called the *Hurlothrumbo.* At the outset, he made a living as an import brokerage businessman and real estate agent. By the early 1850s, he proved himself successful, having amassed a fortune of $250,000, which he lost soon after an attempt to corner the Peruvian rice market. For five years, he disputed the contract in lower courts, eventually reaching the Supreme Court of California. It ruled against Norton.

It remains possible that his legal battle over the rice importation was a cause of his suspicions about elected government that plagued him throughout his "reign."

He declared bankruptcy and left California for a few years. When he returned, it was clear his financial plummet had affected his mental state. In short, he lost his identity.

The first time Norton proclaimed himself "Emperor of these United States" was in letters to the editors of various newspapers and pamphlets, written in response to what he considered ineptitude of the political and legal structures in the United States.

Norton signed them as "Norton I, Emperor of the United States." In September 17, 1859, the editor of the San Francisco Bulletin published one of his announcements as a humor piece. Emperor Norton's first edict was officially dispatched to his subjects.

He began issuing official proclamations, and the editor of the San Francisco Bulletin indulgently continued to publish them. In one imperial edict that October, Norton summoned the United States Army to overthrow Congress. Naturally his orders were ignored by the Army, which did not disturb Congress in any way. In another, he abolished both the Republican and Democratic parties.

In 1860, he declared the republic of the United States dissolved and forbade any members of the (former) congress from assembling. After the onset of the Civil War, he issued a mandate in hopes of solving the country's woes; the mandate ordered the Protestant churches as well as the Roman Catholic Church to recognize him publicly as "Emperor," solving, at least to him, the great divide. After all, an emperor is generally regarded as more powerful than a president, even two presidents.

Rather than trying to depose elected officials after the end of the Civil War in 1865, Norton turned his reforming efforts toward social and political issues. He actively worked to make San Francisco safer, and to increase its national reputation. When he was not issuing decrees and ordering newspapers to print them, he personally inspected his realm.

Imagine a tall, dark-haired, bearded gentleman with a ceremonial sword strapped to his belt and a walking stick or umbrella as his scepter, strolling down San Francisco in a gaudy ceremonial uniform, complete with gold-plated epaulets, a beaver hat on his head. One of his principal missions as emperor was to ensure all sidewalks were clean and unobstructed. In response to what he felt was a lack of respect given to his city, he proclaimed a $25 fine on anyone who uttered "the abominable word

'Frisco', which has no linguistic or other warrant."

Despite his mental instability, Norton displayed a surprisingly profound amount of foresight. Following the Civil War, he instructed nations to form an intergovernmental organization, 50 years before President Wilson founded the League of Nations, and outlawed religious conflicts within the league. He also planned for the construction of a tunnel connection San Francisco to Oakland 60 years prior to the building of the Oakland-San Francisco Bay Bridge.

He even stopped a racist riot. Between 1860 and 1880, anti-Chinese demonstrations broke out in San Francisco's poorer districts. Occasionally rioting broke out and there were fatalities. Legend has it that Emperor Norton placed himself between the Chinese subjects and their harassers, and recited the Lord's Prayer until the crowd dissolved.

Emperor Norton was embraced by the San Francisco citizens, who were touched by his devotion and love of their city. They adopted him and his delusions, humoring him throughout his days. After his financial ruin in the 1850s, Norton could not claim to have a penny to his name. Regardless, his "subjects" took care of him: he regularly enjoyed San Francisco's finest restaurants that commemorated his majesty with bronze plaques hanging in their entryways, and theaters and concert halls did not begin a program without reserving a proper balcony seat or two for him. He appointed citizens to his Imperial Majesty with "seals of approval," which were so prized they boosted trade.

In 1867, Norton was arrested by a policeman who wanted to treat his mental illness. Overnight outrage sparked from citizens and editors, who wrote vicious editorials in their publications. Even the Police Chief became involved when he ordered Norton released. Norton, magnanimously like the ruler he was, granted the policeman an imperial pardon for the mistake.

San Francisco city officials honored him as well. When Norton issued his own money to help pay his debt, the city honored it as accepted local currency. These notes became collector's items. The city replaced his fancy uniform when it looked threadbare with something ostentatious and regal to fit his occupation, which the 1870 U.S. census lists as "Emperor."

On January 8, 1880, Norton died suddenly of apoplexy while walking his daily rounds. The newspapers ran mournful eulogies. One read: "San Francisco without Emperor Norton will be like a throne without a king." Businesses closed; flags hung at half-mast. His funeral was elaborate. Twenty thousand of his former "subjects" attended.

His Imperial Majesty Emperor Norton I

remain the U.S.'s only emperor. Although he was a self-proclaimed ruler, he absolutely suffered from mental illness, and his addition to this list is a charming recess from the more bloodthirsty monarchs.

Genuine Madness and Insanity

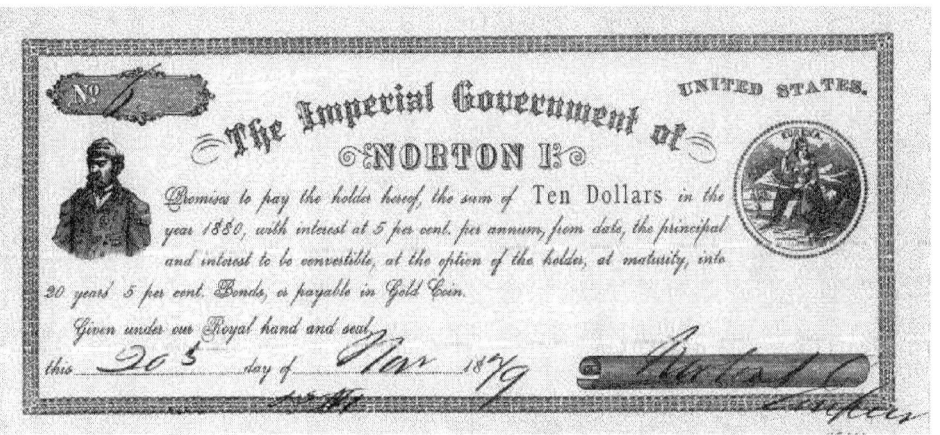

A ten dollar note issued by the Imperial
Government of Norton I

Emperor Norton dressed as the Pope at the funeral of the itinerant dog Lazarus

Ludwig II (1845 - 1886) and Otto (1848 - 1916)

Ludwig II and Otto of Bavaria are a package deal. They were the mad brother-kings of Bavaria during the nineteenth century. Because they both suffered from similar symptoms, many historians believe their mental illness was hereditary.

Similar to King Erik XIV of Sweden, the princes were promising heirs: artistically gifted, intelligent and handsome. Ludwig possessed a more romantic, abstract disposition, which caused him melancholia, but Otto was witty and quick-minded. However, their childhoods were not ideal. They were the sons of King Maximilian II of Bavaria and Marie of Prussia. Because their grandfather, Ludwig I, was forced to abdicate the throne on account of his licentious relationship with Lola Montez, Ludwig II became the Crown Prince of Bavaria at three years old. He was prickly of his position, always demanding that he came first, before his brother Otto. Once he even tied up Otto and threatened to behead him; luckily a court official found them before any serious damage could occur. King Maximilian beat young Ludwig when he misbehaved, and Ludwig resented that Otto was the favorite child, although both brothers felt uncomfortable around their parents. They were avid readers, but the Queen was not interested in reading and their conversations were short and superficial. As a result, the boys became awkward and introverted.

In order to preserve his rich inner life from the cruelty of his tutor, Theodor Basselet de la Rosee, Ludwig learned the effectiveness of secrecy and deception. During this period, he became captivated with German legends. His family was occupying the Hohenschwangau castle, decorated with Grail legends and Swan Knights, and daydreamed to escape reality. According to court chroniclers, Ludwig was gifted at languages, mathematics and history. A voracious reader, Ludwig lost himself in the legends of the Nibelungenlied, Tristan and Isolde and Sir Parsival, inspirations for the fairytale castle he would later construct. Although he was praised for his elegant skills, good looks and courage, he was a lonely, isolated child. Eduard von Bomhard, the Minister of Justice, noted in his memoirs that the Crown Prince had a brilliant but eccentric mind. On one occasion, Ludwig disturbed him by admitting something dark in himself and then returning to his usual charming disposition.

Ludwig II reigned in Bavaria from 1864 almost until his death. One of his first, and certainly most notable, acts after succeeding his father was summoning the infamous composer Richard Wagner to his court in Munich. The king saved Wagner, who had a bad reputation and was in debt, and his career. In turn, Wagner presented him with fantasy works like *Tristan und Isolde* to the delight of the escapist king.

Ludwig patronized other artists as well and introduced the Bavarian people to Ibsen, Weber, Shakespeare and Mozart. Private performances were his favorite. Uncomfortable in public, he attended 209 private performances between 1872 and 1885, including 44 operas, 154 plays and 11 ballets.

Ludwig did not often appear in public or engage with governmental matters. He preferred to day-dream, travel the countryside, commission art and build castles. The most famous is the Schloss Neushwanstein castle, the inspiration for Disney's castle. Perched on the wooded Bavarian mountainside, the interior of Schloss Neushwanstein castle was decorated with some of the king's favorite fantastical frescoes and scenes from Wagner's operas. His castles and palaces are some of the most breathtaking in Europe.

Another one of Ludwig's eccentricities was his refusal to marry. There is speculation he struggled with his sexual orientation. His original diaries, found during WWII, show he tried to suppress his feelings for men.

Conspiracies arose to depose the eccentric king. Bavaria was under severe financial strain; the king was in debt by 14 million marks and had made no attempt to fix this. The ministers were concerned. One created a list of Ludwig's bizarre behaviors, which included his sloppy manners, expensive voyages, violent threats to his servants and general shyness. In June of 1886, a government commission declared King Ludwig deposed and arrested him. In an attempt to flee, the king either committed suicide or was murdered by his enemies. His body was found waist-deep in a lake. Modern historians believe he was murdered, as there was no evidence of water in his lungs to suggest he simply drowned.

His brother Otto succeeded him, with his uncle Luitpold as Regent. By 1872, Otto was classified as mentally ill. In 1875, he stormed into a church service in Munich, dropped to his knees and asked the archbishop for forgiveness of his sins. Afterward he was guarded meticulously. His final public appearance was at a parade in 1875, at his brother's side.

Although the Bavarian cabinet enthroned Otto, he was unable to rule. From 1886 until 1913, he was king in name only, Luitpold king in all but name. When Luitpold died in 1912, his son took regency and the constitution of Bavaria passed an amendment that stated any regent who served for ten years or longer due to the incapacity of the king could proclaim an end to the regency and assume the crown for himself. Otto was deposed the day after, although he retained his titles and honors until his death in 1916. Ludwig III of Bavaria, Luitpold's son, reigned until the end of WWI, when German's monarchies dissolved.

Some of Otto's eccentricities include only

wearing black, standing in corners and gesturing to himself wildly, talking to imaginary people and a preoccupation with lighting matches.

Compared to many other mad monarchs, the brother-kings of Bavaria were melancholic eccentrics rather than tyrannical despots. When writing about her cousin Ludwig II, Empress Elisabeth of Austria claimed he was not mad at all, but merely lived in a world of dreams. Whether Ludwig was insane remains a question posed by modern historians. Some believe he suffered from the effects of chloroform, which at the time was used to treat the pain caused by toothaches. Otto, on the other hand, seems to have exhibited much more obvious signs of mental illness. Whereas Ludwig daydreamed, Otto actively engaged with imaginary phantoms. Regardless of their mismanagement, these monarchs were relatively harmless. Ludwig's lasting contribution, his patronage of art and his gorgeous castles, outweigh his irresponsible management of the realm.

Printed in Great Britain
by Amazon

54347231R00099